Food with Thought

Food with Thought

THE WIT AND WISDOM OF CHINESE FORTUNE COOKIES

collected by

Dr. Edward Mickolus

ISBN-10: 1508796734
ISBN-13: 9781508796732
Library of Congress Control Number: 2015903901
CreateSpace Independent Publishing Platform
North Charleston, South Carolina

Cover photo courtesy of Roseann DeTommaso

For my wife, Susan; daughter, Ciana; and
David Jung and Makoto Hagiwara, who some believe
invented the fortune cookie

What better way to end a meal—from anywhere—than with a fortune? And not just what appears on the bill! Alas, only American-style Chinese restaurants have made post-meal fortunes into a customer favorite. At least 99% (you can check the math by digging through this book's entries if you'd like) are upbeat and positive.

Some say that the American tradition of fortune cookie fortunes was derived from wartime operations. Back when the Chinese rebelled against the Mongol invaders, they hid notes in moon cakes to keep in contact with each other. Moon cakes, made from lotus nut paste, were not considered a delicacy by the Mongols, so the messages were safe from prying Mongol eyes. Other origin stories are less dramatic, attributing the cookies to Japan or to the founder of the Hong Kong Noodle Company in California.

Some cookies offer more than a bland taste and a short message. The other side of the fortune strip can offer suggestions on what numbers to bet in a lottery, and/or teach you a Chinese word of the day, giving the characters, pronunciation, and meaning of the word. You will not find those add-ons here; I'll leave those services to a random number generator and a Chinese language course.

Fortune cookie fortunes can be corny, but can sometimes offer great philosophical insight into the human condition. *Bartlett's Familiar Quotations* often are matched by the wisdom of the anonymous writers of these one-liners. Some of these sentiments can be found on motivational posters; others were perhaps lifted from books of inspirations; still others might have been adapted for or from movies, horoscopes, poems, lyrics, song titles, or seers. We often read these fortunes aloud in a crowd, but sometimes they might merit solitary pondering. I've edited out most of the typos and malapropisms, except when they were crucial to the message. Perhaps you will find this book inspirational, motivational, or at least entertaining.

Finally, in no particular order, here are a few of my favorites:

A diamond is a hunk of coal that stuck with it.

A friend is someone who knows the song in your heart, and can sing it back to you when you have forgotten the words.

A scholar's ink lasts longer than a martyr's blood.

A single kind word will keep one warm for years.

Do not upset the penguin today.

Don't kiss an elephant today.

Don't pursue happiness – create it.

Even the greatest of whales is helpless in the desert.

Failure is success trying to be born.

Failure is the path of least persistence.

It never pays to kick a skunk.

Let no one ever come to you without leaving happier.

Never wear your best pants when you go out to fight for freedom.

None of the secrets of success will work unless you do.

So live that you wouldn't be ashamed to sell the family parrot to the town gossip.

Today you shed your last tear. Tomorrow fortune knocks at your door.

You are an angel. Beware of those who collect feathers.

Your child will have a generous and loving spirit and be cherished by many.

When you expect your opponent to yield, you should also avoid hurting him.

Wise sayings often fall on barren ground, but a kind word is never thrown away.

Word to the wise: Don't play leapfrog with a unicorn…

Table of Contents

Advice 1

Aphorisms 48

Personal Qualities 115

Predictions. 138

Advertisements. 176

Miscellany and Self-Aware Cookies 180

Further Reading 187

About The Author 189

Advice

A good time to finish up old tasks.

A good time to start something new.

A good way to keep healthy is to eat more Chinese food.

A new pair of shoes would do you a world of good.

A pleasant experience is ahead. Don't pass it by.

Accept something that you cannot change, and you will feel better.

Accept the next proposition you hear.

Accept what comes to you each day.

Accept your past without regrets. Handle your present with confidence. Face your future without fear.

Accept yourself.

Act like a role model. The younger is watching.

Adjust finances, make budgets, to improve your standing.

Aim high; time flies.

All things have a cause. Look into your past for answers.

Always begin with an end in mind.

Always accept yourself the way you are.

Always look for ways to add value for the customer.

Always take a photograph of a rainbow when you see one.

Answer just what your heart prompts you.

Anything you do, do it well. The last thing you want is to be sorry for what you didn't do.

Apply yourself to the basics and progress will follow.

Appreciate your own uniqueness and talents.

Ask a friend to join you on your next voyage.

Ask not what your fortune cookie can do for you but what you can do for your fortune cookie.

Ask questions first. Then state your opinions.

Ask yourself if what you are doing today is getting you closer to where you want to be tomorrow.

At this very moment you can change the rest of your life.

Avert misunderstanding by calm, poise and balance.

Avoid taking unnecessary gambles.

Back away from individuals who are impulsive.

Be a generous friend and a fair enemy.

Be alert for new opportunities – pleasure or business.

Be alert, practical and honest.

Be assertive when decisive action is needed.

Be calm when confronting an emergency room crisis.

Be careful and systematic in your business arrangements.

Be careful how you get yourself involved with persons or situations that can't bear inspection.

Be careful in whom you share your confidence.

Be careful not to overspend this month.

Be careful of extravagance.

Be cautious in your financial dealings.

Be direct, usually one can accomplish more that way.

Be efficient with things. With people, be effective.

Be generous, and the favor will be returned.

Be honest and fair to everyone – whether a deeply loved family member or a stranger.

Be mischievous and you will not be lonesome.

Be moderate where pleasure is concerned, avoid fatigue.

Be most affectionate today.

Be nice to people on the way up. You may need them on the way down.

Be on the alert for new opportunities.

Be on the lookout for coming events; they cast their shadows beforehand.

Be patient: in time, even an egg will walk.

Be patient! The Great Wall didn't get built in one day.

Be prepared for extra energy.

Be prepared to modify your plan.

Be proactive, not reactive.

Be secure in the knowledge that you will surely progress.

Be sincere even if you don't mean it.

Be slow in your words and earnest in your conduct. --Confucius

Be strong enough to be creative.

Be tactful; overlook your own opportunity.

Be what you wish others to become.

Become who you are.

Before trying to please others, think of what makes you happy.

Before you wonder "Am I doing things right", ask "Am I doing the right things?"

Begin your life anew with strength, grace, and wonder.

Believe in yourself and you will succeed.

Bend the rod while it is still hot.

Benefit by doing things that others give up on.

Beware of lovers bearing fortune cookies…

Bide your time, for success is near.

Blend receptivity with action.

Change before you have to.

Choose a job you love and you will never need to work. –Confucius

Conceptualize. Organize. Sell. Then do.

Confucius says when prosperity comes, do not use all of it.

Conquer your fears or they will conquer you.

Consolidate rather than expand business projects in the near future.

Consume less. Share more. Enjoy life.

Contact those who share your interest in a project.

Continue - your company is impressed.

Cooperate with those who have both know-how and integrity.

Count your blessings by thinking of those whom you love.

Darkness is only successful when there is no light. Don't forget about light!

Decide what you want and go for it.

Delay it, or drop it.

Demonstrate refinement in everything you do.

Depart not from the path which fate has you assigned.

Discover the power within yourself.

Do everything with confidence.

Do it, delegate it, or delay it.

Do it now! Today will be yesterday tomorrow.

Do not be covered in sadness or be fooled in happiness. They both must exist.

Do not fear what you don't know.

Do not follow where the path may lead. Go where there is no path...and leave a trail.

Do not hesitate to look for help, an extra hand should always be welcomed.

Do not judge a book by its color.

Do not let great ambitions overshadow small successes.

Do not let society paralyze you with its limits.

Do not let what you do not have prevent you from using what you do have.

Do not mistake temptation for opportunity.

Do not rush through life; pause and enjoy it.

Do not seek so much to find the answer as to understand the question better.

Do not think that I or my brothers have supreme control over what will happen to you.

Do not upset the penguin today.

Do something unusual tomorrow.

Do that which your heart tells you.

Do what is right, not what you should.

Do what you want, when you want, and you will be rewarded.

Do you act or react?

Do you feel like you're walking in mud? Take your time today.

Don't ask, don't say. Everything lies in silence.

Don't ask what's in this cookie.

Don't be afraid to take that big step.

Don't be hasty, prosperity will knock on your door soon.

Don't be over self-confident with your first impression of others.

Don't behave with cold manners.

Don't blink. Blink and you're dead.

Don't bother looking for fault. The reward for finding it is low.

Don't control. Enlist support.

Don't count your chickens before they hatch.

Don't cry.

Don't eat any Chinese food today or you'll be sick!

Don't eat any Chinese food today or you'll be very sick!

Don't "face" reality; let it be the place from which you leap.

Don't forget to do good deeds as you accumulate wealth.

Don't hog your knowledge and wisdom.

Don't just spend time; invest it.

Don't kiss an elephant today.

Don't lead if you won't lead.

Don't let doubt and suspicion bar your progress.

Don't let friends impose on you, work calmly and silently.

Don't let the success of Christmas be measured by the money that is spent.

Don't let the past and useless details choke your existence.

Don't let unexpected situations "throw" you.

Don't let your advertisements get ahead of your reality.

Don't live down to expectations. Go out and do something remarkable.

Don't panic.

Don't pursue happiness – create it.

Don't put all your eggs in one basket.

Don't show all your gold at once.

Don't take yourself so seriously, no one else does.

Don't tell all you know but know all you tell.

Don't wait for your ship to come in, swim out to it.

Don't worry about the stock market – invest in family.

Don't worry about the world ending – it's already to-morrow in Australia.

Don't worry about things in the past, there is nothing you can do about them now.

Don't worry about things that are happening now, make the best of a bad situation.

Don't worry about things in the future, they may never happen.

Don't worry. Half the people you know are below average.

Dream lofty dreams, and as you dream, so shall you become.

Dream your dream and your dream will dream of you.

Drive like hell, you will get there.

Eat something you never tried before.

Eat your vegetable and you'll grow up big and strong like Popeye.

Encourage your peers.

Enhance your karma by engaging in various charitable activities.

Enjoy life! It is better to be happy than wise.

Enjoy what you have. Hope for what you lack.

Enjoy yourself while you can.

Enjoyed the meal? Buy one to go, too!

Expect great things and great things will come.

Express yourself; don't hold back!

Face any problem with dignity.

Face facts with dignity.

Failure is not final. Just make sure you don't die because of it.

Find a peaceful place where you can make plans for the future.

Find release from your cares, have a good time.

Finish your work on hand; don't be greedy.

First, become inspired. Then: plan, organize, direct, monitor.

First, understand. Then, be understood.

Focus in on the color yellow tomorrow for good luck!

Follow your dream… take one step at a time, and just continue to climb.

Follow your heart and you'll never get lost.

For better luck you have to wait till autumn.

For each criticism give four compliments.

For success today look first to yourself.

Forgive your enemies, but never forget them.

Forgo confrontations, they will work themselves out.

Fortune not found? Abort, retry, ignore.

Fortune Cookie Says: Care for all things, especially other people.

Gain the courage to change what you can change.

Get off to a new start – come out of your shell.

Get out of the dogma house.

Get ready! Good fortune comes in bunches.

Get your mind set - confidence will lead you on.

Get your mind set in the groove it should follow.

Give a kiss to the person who sits next to you.

Give the world the best you have and the best will come back to you.

Give this to your friend, he may pay for the meal.

Give yourself some peace and quiet for at least a few hours.

Go ask your mom.

Go confidently in the direction of your dreams.

Go hide for a few days.

God can do tremendous things through the person who doesn't care who gets the credit.

God can do wonders with a broken heart if we give Him all the pieces.

God could not be everywhere, therefore He made mothers.

God is rarely early, but always on time.

God never promised us a perfect life. He's saving that for the hereafter.

God will not do for you what you can do for yourself.

Good clothes open many doors. Go shopping.

Grant yourself a wish this year; only you can do it.

Guard against impatience.

Guard well your spare moments. They are like uncut diamonds.

Have a relaxed night tonight.

Have patience – it will benefit you.

Have respect for others and others will, too.

Have the courage and self-respect to accept challenges without being sure you will succeed.

Help improve your neighborhood—move.

Help is always needed but not always appreciated. Stay true to your heart and help those in need whether they appreciate it or not.

Hold on to the past, but eventually, let the times go and keep the memories into the present.

Hone your competitive instincts.

Hope for the best, but prepare for the worst.

If a person who has caused you pain and suffering has brought you, reconsider that person's value in your life.

If love someone a lot tell it before it's too late.

If nothing is pressing, putter around at this or that.

If the idea you had three days ago still looks good, do it!

If you can't be content with what you have received, be thankful for what you have escaped.

If you continually give you will continually have.

If you don't believe Christmas lasts all year, take a look at your charge accounts.

If you don't control your destiny someone else will.

If you don't do it excellently, don't do it at all.

If you don't get everything you want, think of the things you don't get that you don't want.

If you don't have a competitive edge, don't compete.

If you feel you are right, stand firmly by your convictions.

If you have something good in your life, don't let it go!

If you have something worth fighting for, then fight for it.

If you love someone, keep fighting for them.

If you only speak well of others, you never need to whisper.

If you would be loved, love and be lovable.

If your cookie still in one piece, buy lotto.

If your desires are not extravagant they will be granted.

If your friend wants to learn to drive, don't stand in the way.

If your work is not finished, blame it on the computer.

Ignore previous cookie.

In a new situation, get all your expectations on the table.

In case of fire, keep calm, pay bill and run.

In communications, focus your attention on the receiver.

In every enterprise, consider the outcome.

In fair weather, prepare for foul.

In the absence of authority assume it.

Influence someone you do not know.

Innovate or evaporate.

Instead of worrying and agonizing, move ahead constructively.

Invest, but never speculate.

Investigate new possibilities with friends. Now is the time!

It is better to deal with problems before they arise.

It is impossible to please everybody. Please yourself first.

It is not necessary to show others that you have changed; the change will be obvious.

It may be well to consult others before taking unusual action.

It would be best to maintain a low profile for now.

It's a perfect day to give your special someone a gift.

It's about time you asked that special someone on a date.

It's over your head now. Time to get some professional help.

It's the worst of times; you need to summon your optimism.

It's time to get moving. Your spirits will lift accordingly.

Judge not according to the appearance.

Keep in close touch with what your competition is doing.

Keep it simple. The more you say, the less people remember.

Keep this fortune, it'll bring your heart's desires.

Keep true to the dreams of your youth.

Keep your expectations reasonable.

Keep your eye out for someone special.

Keep your eyes open. You never know what you might see.

Keep your face always toward the sunshine and the shadows will fall behind you.

Keep your family traditions alive and flourishing.

Keep your feet on the ground even though friends flatter you.

Keep your goals away from the trolls.

Keep your nose to the grindstone.

Keep your plans secret for now.

Keeping irritability under control would be smart.

Know the right moment.

Know who knows and you need not know.

Learn. Commit. Do. (Repeat forever.)

Learn how to refuse favors, this is a great and useful art.

Learn to laugh at yourself. You'll always be amused.

Let no one ever come to you without leaving happier.

Let not your hand be stretched out to receive and shut when you should repay.

Let the deeds speak.

Let the race begin.

Let the people who do the work design the solutions.

Let there be magic in your smile and firmness in your handshake.

Let your fantasies unwind…

Let your heart make your decisions – it does not get as confused as your head.

Let your imagination wander.

Let your personality shine tonight.

Let's finish this up now; someone is waiting for you on that.

Like the food? Get an extra meal to go.

Listen to everyone. Ideas come from everywhere.

Listen to friends with an ear to the future.

Listen to life, and you will hear the voice of life crying, Be!

Live each day well and wisely.

Live for today. Learn from yesterday. Look to tomorrow.

Live for today – remember yesterday – plan for tomorrow.

Live like you are on the bottom, even if you are on the top.

Live your life as an exclamation, rather than explanation.

Live your life as if you were someone's only role model.

Live your life so that all you want your children to be, they see in you.

Look before you leap. Or wear a parachute.

Look for happiness and you will find it.

Look for new outlets for your own creative abilities.

Look for the big picture.

Look for the dream that keeps coming back.

Look for the good. Search for the truth. Hope for the best.

Look! Good fortune is around you.

Look in the right places and you will find good fortune.

Look right...now look left...now look forward (do this really fast). Do you feel any different? Good, you should feel dizzy.

Look toward the future, but not so far as to miss today.

Look with favor upon a bold beginning.

Love always and deeply.

Love is at your hands. Be glad and hold on to it.

Love thy neighbor, just don't get caught!

Luck is now with you, act upon your instincts.

Lucky you. Get out your party clothes. The clean ones.

Make a wise choice every day.

Make all you can, save all you can, give all you can.

Make amends wherever possible.

Make every minute count.

Make love, not bugs.

Make the system work for you, not the other way around.

Make time for a relaxing vacation.

Make time for prayer and the scriptures in your daily life.

Make two grins grow where there was only a grouch before.

Make your dreams a reality.

Make your life your sermon.

Meet your opponent half way. You need the exercise.

Make yourself necessary to somebody.

Measure how far you've come, not where you came from.

Measure success, not by how much money you make, but by your contributions to the lives of others.

Never bring unhappy feelings into your home.

Never compare yourself to the best others can do, but to the best you can do.

Never cut what you can untie.

Never delegate planning, motivating, and evaluating.

Never despair, but if you do, work on in despair.

Never explain—your friends do not need it, and your enemies will not believe it anyway.

Never forget a friend, especially if he owes you.

Never forget that contentment is the greatest wealth.

Never give up.

Never give up. Always find a reason to keep trying.

Never give up on someone that you don't go a day without thinking about.

Never give up, unless defeat arouses that girl in accounting.

Never give up. You're not a failure if you don't give up.

Never miss a chance to keep your mouth shut.

Never quit!

Never reveal the bottom of your purse or the depth of your mind.

Never say never.

Never tease an armed midget with a high five.

Never throw good money after bad.

Never trouble trouble till trouble troubles you.

Never underestimate the power of the human touch.

Never underestimate the power of the symbolic.

Never upset the driver of the car you're in; they're the master of your destiny until you get home.

Never wear your best pants when you go out to fight for freedom.

Next time, order the shrimp.

Next time you have the opportunity, go on a roller coaster.

Now go to it! It's ready to be picked.

Now is the most precious time. Seize it, live it, because it shall never come again.

Now is the time to make circles with mints, do not haste any longer.

Now is the time to resolve all unfinished business.

Now is the time to start something new.

Now is the time to try something new.

Observe, listen, think, feel, use your intuition – then speak.

Offer justifications, not excuses.

Ok to look at past and future. Just don't stare.

One good way to sell; make it convenient to buy.

Only listen to the fortune cookie; disregard all other fortune telling units.

One always regrets what one could have done. Remember this for next time.

One who admires you greatly is hidden before your eyes.

Open up your heart – it can always be closed again.

Over deliver. Under promise.

Pass the credit. Save the cash.

Pat yourself on the back for making that right choice.

Pay attention to your nonverbal cues, and try turning it down.

Peace comes from within. Seek it from yourself.

Pick another fortune cookie.

Place special emphasis on old friendship.

Plan your journey with God's help, and the ride will be smooth.

Plan your work and work your plan. (And be prepared for the unexpected.)

Plant a sunflower garden this spring!

Postpone all financial decisions for at least a week.

Pray for what you want, but work for the things you need.

Pray to God, but row toward shore.

Prepare today for the demands of tomorrow.

Present your best ideas today to an eager and welcoming audience.

Promote literacy. Buy a box of fortune cookies today.

Put the data you have uncovered to beneficial use.

Put your mind into planning today. Look into the future.

Put your unhappiness aside. Life is beautiful, be happy.

Reach out your hand today to support others who need you.

Read a biography of someone you have always admired.

Reconcile with an old friend. All has been forgotten.

Relax and enjoy yourself.

Rely on close friends to give you advice.

Remember: every downhill has its uphill.

Remember that life's experiences are almost always more valuable than things.

Remember that the happiest people are not those getting more, but those giving more.

Remember that what you do with what happens to you is more important than what happened.

Remember the fate of the early worm.

Remember this: duct tape can fix anything, so don't worry about messing things up.

Remember to keep the holiday spirit when you throw out the Christmas tree.

Remember to share good fortune with friends.

Remember what you receive, not what you give.

Resist the devil and he will flee from you.

Romance stirs your heart—share it with others.

Rome was not built in a day. Be patient.

Run.

See if you can learn anything from the children.

See the beauty in everything.

See the light at the end of the tunnel.

Seek nonviolence in everything you do.

Seek out the significance of your problem at this time. Try to understand.

Seize every second of your life and savor it.

Sell your ideas - they are totally acceptable.

Sell your ideas - they have exceptional merit.

Share your enthusiasm—it will prove infectious.

Share your happiness with others today.

Share your joys and sorrows with your family.

Shoot for the moon! If you miss, you will still be amongst the stars.

Show empathy for your customers.

Show gratitude for what you have now, then for all good things lie ahead.

Silence will be your best reply.

Simplicity and clarity should be the theme in your dress.

Simplicity and clarity should be your theme in dress.

Smile. Tomorrow is another day.

Smile when you are ready.

So live that you wouldn't be ashamed to sell the family parrot to the town gossip.

Some people never have anything except ideas. Go do it.

Someone is looking up to you. Don't let that person down.

Someone is watching you right now, don't turn around.

Speak well of friends. Of enemies, say nothing.

Spread love wherever you go.

Stand for something or you could fall for anything.

Start every day off with a smile. At least it's a good start.

Stay true to those who would do the same for you.

Stay to your inner-self, you will benefit in many ways.

Stop eating now. Food poisoning no fun.

Stop nagging to your partner and take it day by day.

Stop procrastinating – starting tomorrow.

Stop searching forever, happiness is just next to you.

Stop thinking about the road not taken and pave over the one you did.

Stop waiting! Buy that ticket. Take that special trip.

Stop wishing. Start doing.

Suppose you can get what you want.

Take a break and enjoy your life.

Take a minute and let it ride, then take a minute to let it breeze.

Take a trip with a friend.

Take advantage of an unusual opportunity to advance.

Take as long a view as you can afford to take.

Take control of your life rather than letting things happen just like that!

Take no risks with your reputation.

Take one day at a time.

Take pride in everything you do.

Take that chance you've been considering.

Take the chance while you still have the choice.

Take time every day to appreciate the gifts God gives us in people, in nature, in the arts.

Take time to laugh for it is the music of the soul.

Take time to smell the roses.

Take time to stop at the designated "scenic overlooks".

Tell the truth. It's easier to remember.

Tell them before it's too late…

Tell them what you really think. Otherwise, nothing will change.

Tell your best friends how much you appreciate having them in your life.

The best exercise for the heart is to reach down and help others up.

The dream you've been dreaming all your life isn't worth it. Find a new dream, and once you're sure you've found it, fight for it.

The earth is a school; learn in it.

The end is near; might as well have dessert.

The fortune you seek is in another cookie.

The important thing is to express yourself.

The next snowy weekend, get out the board game you enjoyed most growing up.

The one you love is closer than you think.

The smart thing to do is to be yourself.

The smart thing to do is to prepare for the unexpected.

The smart thing is to prepare for the unexpected.

The social scene can be fun today.

The time is right to make new friends.

The way you spend the holidays is much more important than how much you spend.

There is a time to be practical now.

There is no mistake so great as that of being always right.

There is someone annoying in your life that you need to listen to.

Think clearly. Act decisively. Live honorably.

Think win-win or no deal.

This is a good time to consider formally helping others.

This fortune is no good. Try another.

Time is in your favor, be patient.

Time makes one wise. Ask advice from someone older than you.

To build a better world, start in your community.

To clarify another's problem, rephrase the content, reflect the feeling.

To keep the heart unwrinkled, be hopeful, kind, and cheerful. It's the only way to triumph over old age.

To make a good product, design a smart process.

Today, give control over to another person. It is definite.

Today is an ideal time to water your personal garden.

Today, you should be a passenger. Stay close to a driver for a day.

Today, you should spend some time to search in yourself.

Tomorrow Morning, Take a left turn as soon as you leave home.

Tomorrow, take a moment to do something just for yourself.

Traveling more often is important for your health and happiness.

Treasure what you have.

Trust him, but still keep your eyes open.

Trust your intuition.

Trust your intuition. The universe is guiding your life.

Try everything once, even the things you don't think you will like.

Try to channel excess energies into rejuvenation.

Understand that you have the skills and experiences that will equip you for different adventures.

Union gives strength. Work collaboratively.

Unleash your life force.

Use the force.

Use your instincts now.

Use your talents. That's what they are intended for.

Warning, do not eat your fortune.

Whatever your goal is in life, embrace it, visualize it, and it will be yours.

When all else seems to fail, smile for today and just love someone.

When chosen for jury duty, tell judge fortune cookie says, "guilty!"

When fear hurts you, conquer it and defeat it!

When hungry, order more Chinese food.

When in anger, sing the alphabet.

When in doubt, let your instincts guide you.

When the moment comes, take the last one.

When the moment comes, take the last one from the left.

When the moment comes, take the top one.

When you expect your opponent to yield, you should also avoid hurting him.

When you look down, all you see is dirt, so keep looking up.

Whenever possible, keep it simple.

While you have this day, fill it with life. While you're in this moment, give it your own special meaning and purpose and joy.

Word to the wise: Don't play leapfrog with a unicorn…

Work hard. Help others. Be sincere.

Work on improving your exercise routine.

Working hard will make you live a happy life.

Working out the kinks today will make for a better tomorrow.

Yes.

Yes, go ahead with confidence.

You are a person with a good sense of justice. Now it's time to act like it.

You are an angel. Beware of those who collect feathers.

You are capable, competent, and creative. Prove it.

You are extremely loved. Don't worry.

You are thinking about doing something. Don't do it; it won't help anything.

You are what you are; understand yourself before you react.

You can always trust your friends.

You can choose, right now and in every moment, to put your powerful and effective abilities to purposeful use. There is always something you can do, no matter what the situation may be, that will move your life forward.

You don't need the answers to all life's questions. Just ask your father what to do.

You find beauty in ordinary things. Do not lose this ability.

You have found good company. Enjoy.

You have strong personal ideas and convictions. Treasure them.

You know what you want – get to work and make it materialize.

You may be hungry soon; order a takeout now.

You must try, or hate yourself for not trying.

You should learn to read between the lines.

You should not eat food with hands. It will get under fingernails.

You should pay for this check. Be generous.

You will be hungry soon, order takeout now.

You will do well to expand your business.

Your destiny lies before you, choose wisely.

Your father still loves and is always with you. Remember that.

Your intuition is excellent but another viewpoint could be helpful.

Your problem just became your stepping stone. Catch the moment.

Your problem just got bigger. Think, what have you done?

Your smile will tell you what makes you feel good.

Watch your relations with other people carefully, be reserved.

Aphorisms

$ is just a concept. People empower it.

A baby is God's way of saying the world should go on.

A bargain is something you don't need at a price you can't resist.

A beauty is a woman you notice, a charmer is a woman who notices you.

A billionaire's joke is always funny.

A bird in the hand is worth three in the bush!

A clean conscience is a soft pillow.

A clear conscience is usually the sign of a bad memory.

A closed mouth gathers no feet.

A conclusion is simply the place where you got tired of thinking.

A cynic is only a frustrated optimist.

A day of worry is more exhausting than a week of work.

A diamond is a hunk of coal that stuck with it.

A diamond is a piece of coal that stuck with the job.

A difference, to be a difference, must make a difference.

A different world cannot be built by indifferent people.

A dose of adversity is often as needful as a dose of medicine.

A dream will always triumph over reality, once it is given a chance.

A faithful friend is a strong defense.

A fanatic is one who won't change his mind, and won't change the subject.

A feeling is an idea with roots.

A focused mind is one of the most powerful forces in the universe.

A friend asks only for your time not your money.

A friend is a present you give yourself.

A friend is someone who knows the song in your heart, and can sing it back to you when you have forgotten the words.

A gift horse is better than a crazy horse.

A girl who is free for the evening can be one of the most expensive things in the world.

A girlfriend is a bottle of wine; a wife is a wine bottle.

A good evening is one spent in good company.

A good example is the best sermon.

A good home is happiness.

A great pleasure in life is doing what others say you can't.

A handful of patience is worth more than a bushel of brains.

A human being is a deciding being.

A journey of a thousand miles begins with a single step.

A journey must begin with a single step.

A kind word will keep someone warm for years.

A kiss is not a kiss without the heart.

A liar is not believed even though he tells the truth.

A little courtesy will go a long way.

A man without aim is like a clock without hands, as useless if it turns as if it stands.

A merry heart doeth good like a medicine.

A merry heart maketh a cheerful countenance.

A metaphor could save your life.

A modest man never talks of himself.

A new friend helps you break out of an old routine.

A part of us remains wherever we have been.

A perfect statue never comes from a bad mold.

A person travels the world over in search of what he needs and returns home to find it.

A pet will always brighten your day.

A problem is a backwards opportunity.

A quiet evening with friends is the best tonic for a long day.

A scalded cat from cold water runs.

A scholar's ink lasts longer than a martyr's blood.

A sense of humor is the pole that adds balance as you walk the tightrope of life.

A ship in the harbor is safe, but that's not what ships are built for.

A single conversation with a wise man is better than ten years of study.

A single kind word will keep one warm for years.

A small house will hold as much happiness as a big one.

A smile is the shortest distance between two people.

A smile is your personal welcome mat.

A stranger is a friend you have not spoken to yet.

A true friend walks in when the rest of the world walks out.

A truly great person never puts away the simplicity of a child.

A warm smile is testimony of a generous nature.

A well-aimed spear is worth three.

A wise man knows everything.   A shrewd one, everybody.

A wish is what makes life happen when you dream of rose petals.

A woman who seeks to be equal to men lacks ambition.

Acting is not lying. It is finding someone hiding inside you and letting that person run free.

Action speaks nothing, without the Motive.

Actions speak louder than talks.

Adversity is the parent of virtue.

Advice, when most needed, is least heeded.

Affirm it, visualize it, believe it, and it will actualize itself.

After graduation, you enter upon the time of life where you are responsible for grading your own answers.

Age can never hope to win you while your heart is young.

Alas! The onion you are eating is someone else's water lily.

All comes at the proper time to him who knows how to wait.

All events are blessings given to us to learn from.

All fruits have their season.

All great deeds, and all great thoughts, have a ridiculous beginning. Good luck on your journey.

All people smile in the same language.

All progress occurs because people dare to be different.

All the water in the world can't sink a ship unless it gets inside.

All the world may not love a lover but they will be watching him.

All things come to him who goes after them.

All things come to him who waits.

All your fingers can't be of the same length.

Alone we can do little, together we can do so much.

An alarm clock is a device to awaken people who don't have babies.

An angry man opens his mouth and shuts up his eyes.

An empty stomach is not a good political adviser.

An optimist is someone who tells you to cheer up when things are going his way.

An understanding heart warms all that are graced with its presence.

An upward movement initiated in time can counteract fate.

And remember that behind every successful woman… is a basket of dirty laundry.

Anger begins with folly, and ends with regret.

Answers make you wise, but questions make you human.

Any day above ground is a good day.

Any decision you have to make tomorrow is a good decision.

Any fool can criticize. Many do.

Anyone that dares to be, can never be weak.

Anyone who dares to be, can never be weak.

Appearances are often deceiving.

As is the mother, so is her daughter.

As the purse is emptied, the heart is filled.

As trust increases, so, too, does efficiency.

Aside from survival, most people want to be understood.

At times it is better to know when to exit than to enter.

At 20 years of age the will reigns; at 30 the wit; at 40 the judgment.

Attitude more than aptitude will determine your altitude.

Babies are angels whose wings grow shorter as their legs grow longer.

Babies are Mother Nature's way of saying there is more to life than sleep.

Baby – a little person who is subject to change without notice.

Bad habits are hard to break, especially if you like them.

Beauty is simply beauty; originality is magical.

Becoming a mother is to decide forever to have your heart go walking around outside your body.

Before the beginning of great brilliance, there must be chaos.

Before honor is humility.

Before receiving honor, you must have humility.

Before you can be reborn you must die.

Behind an able man, there are always other able men.

Behind bad luck comes good luck.

Being alone and being lonely are two different things.

Being faithful to a trust brings its own reward.

Being happy is not always being perfect.

Being influenceable is key to influencing others.

Believing is doing.

Believing that you are beautiful will make you appear beautiful to others around you.

Better to be the head of a chicken than the tail of an ox.

Birds are entangled by their feet and men by their tongues.

Birthdays are merely mind over matter. If you don't mind, it doesn't matter!

Blessed are the children for they shall inherit the national debt.

Blessed are the risk takers for they shall bring us tomorrow.

Bread today is better than cake tomorrow.

Broke is only temporary; poor is a state of mind.

Business is not busy-ness.

Change your thoughts and you change the world.

Cheap things are of no value; valuable things are not cheap.

Children are life's reward.

Circumstance does not make the man; it reveals him to himself.

Cleaning house while your kids are growing up is like shoveling snow before it stops snowing.

Communication is the currency of leadership.

Communication is your most important source of power.

Compassion is a way of being.

Compassion will cure more than condemnation.

Compliments cost nothing yet can give so much.

Confessions: Good for the soul, bad for the reputation.

Confucius say: If you're going to sum up your whole life on this little bit of paper, you're crazy.

Confucius say: Lovers in triangle not on square.

Confucius say: Man who studies hard lives prosperous life.

Confucius say: Man with college degree is one smart cookie!

Confucius say: Show-off always shown up in showdown.

Constant grinding can turn an iron rod into a needle.

Consultant: one who looks at your watch and tells you the time.

Courtesy is contagious.

Customer service is like taking a bath; you have to keep doing it.

Cycles tend to become self-perpetuating.

Delay is the antidote for anger.

Determination is the wake-up call to the human will.

Difficulty at the beginning usually means ease at the end.

Digital circuits are made from analog parts.

Diligence is the mother of good fortune.

Dogs have owners, cats have staff.

Domestic peace is the luxury you enjoy between the baby's bedtime and your own.

Each day comes bearing gifts.

Each day comes just once in a lifetime, today you are creating tomorrow's memories.

Economy is the wealth of the poor and the wisdom of the rich.

Emotion is energy in motion.

Emotions can be sweet and sour, so can your meal.

Ethos/Credibility, Pathos/Empathy, Logos/Logic. You need all three.

Even if the person who appears most wrong, is also quite often right.

Even the greatest of whales is helpless in the desert.

Even the smartest person can learn something from the dumbest.

Every artist was first an amateur.

Every baby comes with the message that God is not yet discouraged.

Every day is a new day. But tomorrow is never promised.

Every excess becomes a vice.

Every exit is an entrance to new experiences.

Every friend joys in your success.

Every man is a volume if you know how to read him.

Every person is the architect of his or her own fortune.

Every truly great accomplishment is at first impossible.

Every woman is at heart a mother; every man is at heart a bachelor.

Everyone excels at something in which another fails.

Everything happens for a reason.

Everything has beauty but not everyone sees it.

Everything we have we owe to God.

Excellence is the difference between what I do and what I am capable of.

Excuses are easy to manufacture, and hard to sell.

Expect nothing and you will never be disappointed.

Expectation is often better than realization.

Experience is a wonderful thing. It enables you to recognize a mistake when you make it again.

Experience is the mama of Science.

Failure is not defeat until you stop trying.

Failure is success trying to be born.

Failure is the mother of all success.

Failure is the only opportunity to begin again more intelligently.

Families are like fudge… mostly sweet with a few nuts.

Family is more valuable than money.

Fear can keep us up all night long, but faith makes one fine pillow.

Fear of failure is the biggest obstacle to success.

Fear is just excitement in need of an attitude adjustment.

Fear is the darkroom where negatives are developed.

First they ignore you, then they attack you, then you win.

Follow your bliss and the Universe will open doors where there were once only walls.

For a good cause, wrongdoing may be virtuous.

For hate is never conquered by hate. Hate is conquered by love.

For the wise man, every day is a festival.

Fortune favors the brave.

Fortune said a palm can say a lot. Especially when it smacks.

Fortune truly helps those who are of good judgment.

Free advice is usually worth what you paid for it.

Freed from desire, then you can see the hidden mystery.

Friendship is an ocean that you cannot see bottom.

Friendships are made, not discovered.

From listening comes wisdom and from speaking repentance.

Functioning superbly should come automatically.

Funny thing about humility. Just when you think you've got it, you've lost it.

Give a person a fish, he'll eat for a day. Teach a person to fish, he always smells funny.

Go with the flow will make your transition ever so much easier.

God has given you one face, and you make yourselves another.

Good beginning is half done.

Good ideas come free of charge.

Good luck is the result of good planning.

Good negotiators separate people from problems.

Good. Fast. Cheap. (Pick two.)

Good sense is the master of human life.

Good things take time.

Good-humor is goodness and wisdom combined.

Graduation is not the end; it's the beginning.

Grand adventures await those who are willing to turn the corner.

Great knowledge brings great things.

Great thoughts come from the heart.

Great works are performed not by strength, but by perseverance.

Habitual patterns of thought determine success or failure.

Half of being smart is knowing what you are dumb about.

Half the world knows how the other half ought to live.

Happiness comes from a good life.

Happiness is an activity.

Happiness is not the absence of conflict, but the ability to cope with it.

Happiness is often a rebound from hard work.

Happiness isn't something you remember, it's something you experience.

Hard words break no bones, fine words butter no parsnips.

Hard work reaps rewards.

He who climbs a ladder must begin at the first step.

He who dies with the most toys, still dies.

He who hurries cannot walk with dignity.

He who knows that enough is enough will always have enough.

He who knows the most says the least.

He who laughs at himself never runs out of things to laugh at.

He who laughs last is laughing at you.

He who loves you will follow you.

He who never makes mistakes never did anything that's worthy.

He who slithers among the ground is not always a foe.

He who sows courtesy reaps friendship, and he who plants kindness gathers love.

He who throws dirt is losing ground.

He who throws mud loses ground.

Hearty laughter is a good way to jog internally without having to go outdoors.

Hell is paved with good intentions.

Helping a friend is like helping yourself.

Holiday time is when people want the past forgotten and their present remembered.

Honesty and integrity are some of the best attributes.

Honesty is the best policy.

Honor is your greatest reward.

Hope brings about a better future.

Hope is like a balloon… it can't soar to the heavens if you hold it by the string.

Hope is like food. You will starve without it.

How can you have a beautiful ending with making beautiful mistakes?

How dark is dark? How wise is wise?

How wonderful it is that nobody need wait a single moment to improve the world.

Human evolution: "wider freeway" but narrow viewpoints.

Human invented language to satisfy the need to complain.

Humor is an affirmation of dignity.

Humor usually works at the moment of awkwardness.

I hear and I forget. I see and I remember. I do and I understand.

Ideas are like children: there are none so wonderful as your own.

Idleness is the holiday of fools.

If it ain't broken, don't fix it.

If it seems the fates are against you today, they probably are.

If the eyes are looked upon as the windows to the soul, then a smile must be the doorway to the heart.

If the profits are great, the risks are great.

If the shoe fits, it's probably your size.

If winter comes, can spring be far behind?

If you're happy, you're successful.

If you are afraid to shake the dice, you will never throw a six.

If you are never patient, you will never get anything done.

If you believe you can do it, you will be rewarded with success.

If you can learn from failure, you'll be able to lead the way.

If you continually give, you will continually have.

If you don't give something, you will not get anything.

If you eat a box of fortune cookies, anything is possible.

If you have tried to do something and failed, you are vastly better off than if you tried to do nothing and succeeded.

If you love someone enough and they break your heart, you can't stop yourself from still loving them again even after all that pain.

If you never expect anything, you can never be disappointed.

If you never give up on love, it will never give up on you.

If you throw nuts at a squirrel it will throw them back.

If you want the rainbow, then you have to tolerate the rain.

If you wish to know the mind of a man, listen to his words.

Ignorance never settles a question.

Impossible is a word only to be found in the dictionary of fools.

Impossible standards just make life difficult.

In a good business deal everyone wins.

In agreements, written words help dispel doubt.

In everything there is a piece of truth. But a piece.

In God we trust.

In God we trust; all others must pay cash.

In human endeavor, chance favors the prepared mind.

In jealousy there is more self-love than love.

In music, one must think with his heart and feel with his brain.

In order to succeed, we must first believe that we can.

In the cookies of life, friends are the chocolate chips.

In the eyes of lovers, everything is beautiful.

In this life it is not what we take up, but what we give up, that makes us rich.

In this life, we cannot do great things, we can only do small things with great love.

In words of love a little exaggeration is ok.

In youth and beauty, wisdom is rare.

Infant care is a thing that can be learned from the bottom up!

Infinite patience produces immediate results.

Integrity is doing the right thing, even if nobody is watching.

Integrity is the essence of everything successful.

Integrity is the spine of business.

Intelligence is the door to freedom and alert attention is the mother of intelligence.

Investment knowledge pays the best dividends.

It could be better, but it's good enough.

It is best to act with confidence, no matter how little right you have to it.

It is better to be a leader than a follower.

It is better to be the hammer than the anvil.

It is better to be the hammer than the nail.

It is better to have a hen tomorrow than an egg today.

It doesn't matter. Who is without a flaw?

It is easier to resist at the beginning than at the end.

It is good to know that things are improving.

It is much easier to be critical than to be correct.

It is much easier to look for the bad, than it is to find the good.

It is much wiser to take advice than to give it.

It is never too late. Just as it is never too early.

It is not good to be a user. Blessings come from being a giver, not a taker.

It is now, and in this world, that we must live.

It is often better not to see an insult than to avenge it.

It never pays to kick a skunk.

It takes more than good memory to have good memories.

It takes ten times as many muscles to frown as it does to smile.

It's amazing how much good you can do if you don't care who gets the credit.

It's better to be alone sometimes.

It's a good thing that life is not as serious as it seems to the waiter.

It's alright to have butterflies in your stomach.   Just get them to fly in formation.

It's kind of fun to do the impossible.

It's never crowded along the "extra mile".

It's never too late for good things to happen!

It's nice to be remembered, but it's far cheaper to be forgotten.

Jealousy doesn't open doors, it closes them!

Jealousy is a useless emotion.

Joys are often the shadows, cast by sorrows.

Judgment comes from experience. Experience comes from bad judgment.

Labels are for cans not people.

Land is always in the mind of flying birds.

Laughter is the music of a happy heart.

Laughter is the shortest distance between two people.

Lend your money and lose your friend.

Life always gets harder near the summit.

Life begins at forty!

Life begins at the end of your comfort zone.

Life consists not in holding good cards, but in playing those you hold well.

Life is a blank canvas. You choose what to paint on it.

Life is a cup to be filled not drained.

Life is a tragedy for those who feel and a comedy for those who think.

Life is a verb.

Life is like a dogsled team. If you ain't the lead dog, the scenery never changes.

Life is like juggling knives, everyone can tell when you've messed up.

Life is not the candle or the wick, it's the burning.

Life is too short to be little.

Life is too short to hold grudges.

Life is too short to waste time hating anyone.

Life is what happens to you while you're busy eating birthday cake.

Like the river flow into the sea. Some things are just meant to be.

Little and often makes much.

Looking fifty is great – if you're sixty!

Love asks me no questions, and gives me endless support. Shakespeare

Love because it is the only true adventure.

Love begets love.

Love can last a lifetime, if you want it to.

Love can turn a cottage into a golden palace.

Love conquers all.

Love does not always wear a friendly face.

Love is as necessary to human beings as food and shelter.

Love is blind. Jealousy sees too much.

Love is blind to the future.

Love is for the lucky and the brave.

Love is free. Lust will cost you everything you have.

Love is like a sweet nectarine, good to the last drop.

Love is like the moon, when it does not increase it decreases.

Love is like war, easy to begin, but very hard to stop.

Love is like wildflowers…it is often found in the most unlikely places.

Love is the glue that holds together everything in the world.

Love is the only medicine for a broken heart.

Love takes practice.

Love will lead the way.

Low overhead + high demand = sleepful nights.

Man is born to live and not prepare to live.

Man who wear flat board on head may walk down path with dress on and people will applaud.

Man with foot in mouth has athlete's tongue.

Many a false step is made by standing still.

Many answers are questionable.

Many folks are about as happy as they make up their minds to be.

Many people fail because they quit too soon.

Many people who have power become a deaf-mute.

Many questions are unanswerable.

Many receive advice, only the wise profit by it.

Marriage is a lottery, but you cannot tear up your ticket if you lose.

Marriage lets you annoy one special person for the rest of your life.

Marriage is one subject on which all women agree and all men disagree.

Maturity is reached by learning to accept imperfection.

Maxim for life: You get treated in life the way you teach people to treat you.

Meeting adversity well is the source of your strength.

Men are what their mothers made them.

Men do not fail. They give up trying.

Men play the game, but women know the score.

Middle age is having a choice between two temptations and choosing the one that'll get you home earlier.

Middle age is the awkward period when Father Time catches up with Mother Nature.

Middle age is when your classmates are so gray, wrinkled and bald they don't recognize you.

Middle age: when you begin to exchange your emotions for symptoms.

Money flows toward good ideas.

Money seeks good ideas.

Mothers hold their children's hands for a short time, but their hearts forever.

Movies have pause buttons, friends do not.

Much more grows in the garden than that which is planted there.

Nature, time and patience are the three great physicians.

Never regret anything that made you smile.

No distance is too far, if two hearts are tied together.

No man is without enemies.

No one ever went bankrupt because of low overhead.

No one's been hurt from laughing too much.

No person was ever honored for what he received. Honor has been the reward for what he gave.

No problem leaves you where you found it.

Nobody is counting calories at your birthday – they're all too busy counting candles.

None of the secrets of success will work unless you do.

Not all closed eye is sleeping, nor open eye is seeing.

Not having a goal is more to be feared than not reaching one.

Not to decide is a decision.

Nothing astonishes men so much as common sense and plain dealing.

Nothing creates a firmer belief in heredity than a good-looking baby!

Nothing happiness unless first a dream.

Nothing in the world is accomplished without passion.

Nothing in the world is more dangerous than sincere ignorance.

Nothing interferes with the holidays more than looking for a parking space.

Nothing is as good or bad as it appears.

Nothing makes us more tolerant of a neighbor's holiday party than being invited to it.

Nothing seems to make a child more affectionate than sticky hands.

Nothing shows a man's character more than what he laughs at.

Now these three remain, faith, hope and love. The greatest of these is love.

Nowadays in business learning never ends.

Of all the rights of women, the greatest is to be a mother.

Of all the things you wear, your expression is the most noticeable.

Old dreams never die, they just get filed away.

Old friends make best friends.

Old friends, old wines and old gold are best.

On ordinary days, we need to say thanks to God for His gifts to us.

On the right track, means need to run even faster, or get run over.

One generation plants the trees; another gets the shade.

One is not old until regrets take place of dreams.

One joy will scatter a hundred sorrows.

One must know that there is a path at the end of the road.

One of the best ways to persuade others is with your ears – by listening to them.

One who steals honey should beware of the sting.

Only a fool seeks wisdom in dessert.

Only love lets us see normal things in an extraordinary way.

Only talented people get help from others.

Only the educated are free.

Opportunities surround you if you know where to look.

Optimists build castles in the sky.

Others need not lose for you to win.

Our deeds determine us, as much as we determine our deeds.

Our duty, as men and women, is to proceed as if limits to our ability did not exist.

Our first and last love is... self-love.

Our perception and attitude toward any situation will determine the outcome.

Out of confusion come new patterns.

Out of debt, out of danger.

Over every mountain there is a path, although it may not be seen from the valley.

Over self-confidence is equal to being blind.

Over the hill: When you stop describing symptoms, and accept what is chronically wrong.

Pardon is the choicest flower of victory.

Patience is the best remedy for every trouble.

Patience is a key to joy.

Patience is a virtue, unless it's against a brick wall.

Patience is bitter but its fruit is sweet.

Patience is the key to joy.

People are not persuaded by what we say but rather by what they understand.

People buy on emotion and justify with fact.

People tend to get what they expect.

People who are late are often happier than those who have to wait for them.

Person who argues with idiot is taken for fool.

Person who eat fortune cookie gets lousy dessert.

Person who rests on laurels gets thorn in backside.

Pessimists dig dungeons.

Politeness costs nothing and gains everything.

Poverty is no disgrace.

Procrastination… the thief of time.

Products are merely physical expressions of ideas.

Prosperity makes friends and adversity tries them.

Punctuality is the politeness of kings and the duty of gentle people everywhere.

Pure religion is Love in action.

Purposeful prior planning prevents poor performance.

Push will get you far, but pull will get you farther.

Q: What is contained in everything? A: Wisdom.

Q: What is KMS? A: Keep Mouth Shut, the golden rule.

Quality service is what your customers say it is.

Questions provide the key to unlocking our unlimited potential.

Reading to the mind is what exercise is to the body.

Real business often happens after lunch or dinner.

Real business often happens during lunch or dinner.

Real fortune is being heard.

Reforms like charity should begin at home.

Retirement does not mean quitting life.

Rivers need springs.

Run in mud with bare feet, then your feet will be muddy.

Satisfied customers are your best advertisements.

Save money and money will save you.

Second thoughts are often wiser than first impressions.

Seldom in doubt, frequently in error.

Service is the rent we pay for room on this Earth.

Service is the rent we pay for the privilege of living on this planet.

Seven days without prayer makes one weak.

Silence is a virtual.   Especially Dinner time, from telemarketers.

Simple pleasures are the best.

Simplicity of character is the natural result of profound thought.

Sir Winston Churchill: Destiny is not a matter of chance, it is a matter of choice.

Skill comes from diligence.

Sleep is something that science can't abolish – but babies can.

Slow and steady wins the race.

Smiling often can make you look and feel younger.

Some fortune cookies contain no fortune.

Some men dream of fortunes; others dream of cookies.

Some people must break before becoming whole.

Someone once said, if you want to make God laugh, tell Him your plans.

Sometimes the object of the journey is not the end, but the journey itself.

Sometimes travel to new places leads to great transformation.

Sometimes you just need to lay on the floor.

Strong and bitter words indicate a weak cause.

Success is assured when everyone pitches in with a will.

Success is in the details.

Success is not a destiny, it is a journey.

Success is preparation meeting opportunity.

Success is the sum of my unique visions realized by the sweat of perseverance.

Sunshine through hasty news to chase away your blues.

Tact is the art of making a point without making an enemy.

Talking does not teach.

Teamwork: the fuel that allows common people attain uncommon results.

Tears are water for the soul.

That which is genuine needs no explanation.

That which needs to be proved cannot be worth much.

The attitude within is more important than the circumstances without.

The beginning of wisdom is to desire it.

The best holiday gifts are wrapped in smiles.

The best holiday present is a welcome to family and friends.

The best mirror is a good friend.

The best possible infant care is to keep one end full and the other end dry.

The best profit of future is the past.

The best prophet of the future is the past.

The best things in life aren't things.

The best way to give credit is to give it away.

The best way to predict the future is to create it.

The best year-round temperature is a warm heart and a cool head.

The Buddha said there is no one thing stays the same during this life.

The cooler you think you are the dumber you look.

The counting of years matters little, it what we put into the years that gives the meaning.

The cure for grief is movement.

The cycle of life is no reason to be going in circles.

The days that make us happy make us wise.

The days you work are the best days.

The desire of love is to give. The desire of lust is to get.

The early bird gets the worm, but the second mouse gets the cheese.

The eyes believe themselves; the ears believe other people.

The face of nature reflects all of life's ups and downs.

The finest holiday gift to give yourself is a little peace of mind when the season gets hectic.

The finest men like the finest steels have been tempered in the hottest furnace.

The first great gift we can bestow on others is a good example.

The first step to better times is to imagine them.

The four basic food groups during the holiday season are cookies, pastries, ginger bread houses and pies.

The four D's of business: dreams, deals, details, deadlines.

The future belongs to those who believe in the beauty of their dreams.

The future is made of the same stuff as the present.

The gift is not as precious as the thought.

The gifts you have received in life, are the gifts you are here in this world to share.

The great fault in women is to desire to be like men.

The great man is he who dares not lose his child's heart.

The great pleasure in life is doing what people say you cannot do.

The greater part of inspiration is perspiration.

The greatest love is a mother's, then a dog's, then a sweetheart.

The greatest precept is continual awareness.

The greatest risk is not taking one.

The greatest things are done by the aid of small ones.

The greatest war sometimes isn't on the battlefield but against oneself.

The harder you try to not be like your parents, the more likely you will become them.

The harder you work, the luckier you get.

The heart has reasons the mind cannot understand.

The heart is wiser than the intellect.

The heart of a mother is a deep abyss at the bottom of which you will always find forgiveness.

The holiday season is as meaningful as we make it.

The holidays are a great reason to eat too much.

The holidays are a race to see what gives out first – your feet or your money.

The holidays are a time when we eat 2,000 calories before noon.

The human spirit is stronger than anything that can happen to it.

The important thing is to never stop questioning.

The joyfulness of a man prolongeth his days.

The law of heredity is: All undesirable traits come from the other parent.

The laws sometimes sleep, but never die.

The leader seeks to communicate his vision to his followers.

The leaders sense and transform the needs of followers.

The majority of the word "can't" is can.

The man on top of the mountain did not fall there.

The man who rows the boat generally doesn't have time to rock it.

The man who waits till tomorrow, misses the opportunities of today.

The measure of time to your next goal is the measure of your discipline.

The most important thing a father can do for his children is to love their mother.

The most important thing in communication is to hear what isn't being said.

The most useless energy is trying to change what and who God so carefully created.

The most wasted of all days is one without laughter.

The mother's heart is the child's schoolroom.

The old believe everything, the middle-aged suspect everything, the young know everything.

The one good thing about repeating your mistakes is that you know when to cringe.

The only certainty is that nothing is certain.

The only good is knowledge and the only evil ignorance.

The only normal people are the ones you don't know very well.

The only rose without a thorn is friendship.

The only sure thing about luck is that it will change.

The only thing we can give our children is what we are, not what we have.

The only way to have a friend is to be one.

The past is gone... tomorrow is full of possibilities.

The philosophy of one century is the common sense of the next.

The phrase is follow your dreams, not dream period.

The philosophy of one century is common sense to the next.

The physician heals, nature makes well.

The pleasure of what we enjoy is lost by wanting more.

The problem with resisting temptation is that it may never come again.

The purpose of education is to turn mirrors into windows.

The quick fix is a mirage.

The race is not always to the swift, but to those who keep on running.

The road to knowledge begins with the turn of the page.

The road to riches is paved with homework.

The road to success is always under construction.

The road to success is not a path you find but a trail you blaze.

The secret of getting ahead is getting started.

The secret of staying young is good health and lying about your age.

The smallest seed of faith is better than the largest fruit of happiness.

The sun is always shining somewhere.

The superior man is modest in his speech, but he exceeds in his actions.

The tassel is worth the hassle!

The time is always right to do what is right.

The truly educated never graduate.

The two hardest things in life are failure and success.

The ultimate test of a relationship is to disagree but to hold hands.

The way to a man's heart is to his stomach.

The will of the people is the best law.

The wise are aware of their treasure, while fools follow their vanity.

The world is always ready to receive talent with open arms.

The world may be your oyster, but that doesn't mean you'll get its pearl.

The worst of friends may become the best of enemies, but you will always find yourself hanging on.

There are lessons to be learned by listening to others.

There are no limitations to the mind except those we acknowledge.

There are 365 days in a year, may all 365 of your dreams come true.

There are two ways of spreading light: to be the candle or the mirror that reflects it.

There is always a way – if you are committed.

There is no cosmetic for beauty like happiness.

There is no fear for the one whose thought is not confused.

There is no fear in love, but perfect love casteth out fear.

There is no greater pleasure than seeing your loved ones prosper.

There is no grief which time does not lessen and soften.

There is no limit to love's forbearance, to its trust, its hope, its power to endure.

There is no sorrow in the world that a hot bath won't help, just a little bit.

There is nothing that costs so little nor goes so far as courtesy.

There is something seeing and there is something being seen.

There's no such thing as an ordinary cat.

Things are never quite the way they seem.

Things are only impossible until they are not.

Things may come to those who wait, but only the things left by those who hustle.

Think you can. Think you can't. Either way, you'll be right.

Thirty is a nice age for a woman (especially if she happens to be 40)!

Thirty-five is when you finally get your head together and your body starts falling apart.

This is really a lovely day. Congratulations!

This sentence is false. The previous sentence is true.

Those grapes you cannot taste are always sour.

Those who bring sunshine to the lives of others cannot keep it from themselves.

Those who have love, have wealth beyond measure.

Those who never ask know all, or nothing.

Those who walk in others' tracks leave no footprints.

Three can keep a secret, if you get rid of two.

Time is precious, but truth is more precious than time.

Time is the iron that smoothes away the wrinkles in our past.

Time is the wisest counselor.

Time is wealth. Especially with your lawyer.

Time may fly by, but memories don't.

To affect the quality of the day is no small achievement.

To affirm is to make firm.

To be old and wise, you must first be young and stupid.

To courageously shoulder the responsibility of one's mistake is character.

To determine whether someone is beautiful is not by looking at his/her appearance, but his/her heart.

To forgive others one more time is to create one more blessing for yourself.

To give you must receive. To receive you must give.

To keep a lamp burning, we have to keep putting oil in it.

To know how to grow old is the master work of wisdom.

To love is to forgive.

To make the cart go, you must grease the wheels.

To one who waits, a moment seems a year.

To truly find yourself you should play hide and seek alone.

Today is probably a huge improvement over yesterday.

Tomorrow is two days late for yesterday's work.

Too many people volunteer to carry the stool when it's time to move the piano.

True happiness comes from within.

True wisdom is found in happiness.

Trust is your best weakness.

Truth is an unpopular subject, because it is unquestionably correct.

Truth is usually better than subtlety.

Try? No! Do or do not, there is no try.

Two can live as cheaply as one, for half as long.

Two small jumps are sometimes better than one big leap.

Until someone sells an idea nothing happens.

Virtuous find joy while Wrongdoers find grief in their actions.

Vision is the art of seeing what is invisible to others.

Voltaire: No problem can stand the assault of sustained thinking.

We all have extraordinary coded within us, waiting to be released.

We all smile in the same language.

We are here to love each other, serve each other and uplift each other.

We can learn from everyone, especially from our enemies.

We cannot change the direction of the wind, but we can adjust our sails.

We cannot direct the wind but we can adjust the sails.

We can't help everyone. But everyone can help someone.

We could learn a lot from crayons: Some are sharp, some are pretty, some have weird names, and all are different colors. But they all have to learn to live in the same box.

We do not know what the future holds, but we have each other.

We do not remember days, we remember moments.

We feel close to everyone during the holidays – especially in the aisles of stores.

We must always have old memories and young hopes.

We never know the love of the parent until we become parents ourselves.

We spend our school days yearning to graduate and our remaining days nostalgic about our days in school.

Wealth is a state of mind.

Wealth without wisdom is a fool's paradise.

Well-arranged time is the surest sign of a well-arranged mind.

What breaks in a moment may take years to mend.

What comes from the heart, touches the heart.

What ends on hope does not end at all.

What goes around comes around.

What is valuable is not new but what is new is not valuable.

What many of us want for Christmas is – the day after.

What most people consider a virtue, after the age of 40, is simply a loss of energy.

What you don't owe won't hurt you.

What you think is a problem is an opportunity for growth.

What's vice today may be virtue tomorrow.

When fire and water go to war, water always wins.

When it is not necessary to make a decision, it is necessary not to make a decision.

When one cannot invent, one must at least improve.

When one must, one can.

When you can't naturally feel upbeat, it can sometimes help to act as if you did.

When you get something for nothing, you just haven't been billed for it yet.

When you squeeze an orange, orange juice comes out – because that's what's inside.

Where profit is, loss is hidden nearby.

Where there is a will, there is a way.

While too much food may fill the stomach, too much knowledge can never fill the brain.

Willing compromise is the key to gaining unity.

Winners never quit. Quitters never win.

Wisdom is only found in truth.

Wise husband is one who thinks twice before saying nothing.

Wise men learn more from fools than fools from the wise.

Wise sayings often fall on barren ground, but a kind word is never thrown away.

Wishing for the good old days only means you're old.

Without the help of God, we would have nothing.

Words must be weighed and not counted.

Words, once spoken, cannot be recalled.

Work is play. Play is work.

Worries are prayers for outcomes you don't want.

Wrinkles merely indicate where the smiles have been.

You are not judged by the efforts you put in; you are judged on your performance.

You are only as old as you feel.

You can always find happiness at work on Friday.

You can never be certain of success, but you can be certain of failure if you never try.

You can still love what you cannot have in life.

You can't buy experience on the easy payment plan.

You can't go down the right path without first discovering the path to go down.

You cannot become rich except by enriching others.

You cannot demonstrate an emotion or prove an aspiration.

You cannot love life until you live the life you love.

You create your own stage…the audience is waiting.

You don't get harmony when everyone sings the same note.

You don't need talent to gain experience.

You may be disappointed if you fail, but you are doomed if you don't try.

You think that is a secret, but it never has been one.

You try hard, never to fail. You don't, never to win.

You will be wise not to seek too much from others.

You'll never leave the place that's closest to your heart.

Your family is a link to the past, a bridge to the future.

Your fortune is not something to find but to unfold.

Your good deeds are never forgotten.

Your happiness is a byproduct of an effort to make someone else happy.

Your heart is a place to draw true happiness.

Your life does not get better by chance, it gets better by change.

Your pain is the breaking of the shell that encloses your understanding.

Your success depends on your ability to dream and how you follow through.

Your success in life must be earned with earnest efforts.

Personal Qualities

A diversity of friends is a credit to your flexible nature.

A happy and harmonious family is important to you.

A sense of humor is one of your greatest assets.

All of your baby's best traits must come from you.

Among the lucky, you are the chosen one.

Anyone who says things are in bad shape nowadays, hasn't seen you lately.

Are your legs tired? You've been running through someone's mind all day long.

Beauty in its various forms appeals to you.

Because of your melodic nature, the moonlight never misses an appointment.

Confucius say you have a heart as big as Texas.

Courage and optimism are your best traits.

Culture and customs of China attract you.

Even though it will often be difficult and complicated, you know you have what it takes to get it done.

Every friend joys in your success.

Everyone agrees you are the best.

Everyone feels lucky for having you as a friend.

Excitement and intrigue follow you closely wherever you go!

Executive ability is prominent in your make up.

Generosity and perfection are your everlasting goals.

Good things are being said about you.

If everyone is a worm, you should be a glow worm.

If you can read this, you are literate. Congratulations.

Life is a dance floor; you are the DJ!

Life to you is a bold and dashing responsibility.

Life to you is a dashing and bold adventure.

Many admire your social and physical appearance.

Marriage is something you have to give your whole mind to.

No one reads your blog.

Nothing seems impossible to you.

Others enjoy your company.

Others find your charm irresistible.

People admire you for being such a charmer.

People are naturally attracted to you.

People enjoy having you around. Appreciate this.

People find it difficult to resist your persuasive manner.

People find you attractive, inside and out.

Perhaps you've been focusing too much on spending.

Perhaps you've been focusing too much on that one thing.

Rarely do great beauty and great virtue dwell together as they do in you.

Rest has a peaceful effect on your physical and emotional health.

Right now there's an energy pushing you in a new direction.

Self-improvement is a gift you give others.

Some pursue happiness; you create it.

Someone has Googled you recently.

Someone is secretly in love with you.

Someone is speaking well of you.

Someone is thinking of you.

Someone is watching you from afar.

Someone special is thinking of you.

Someone thinks you are very special and wants to let you know it.

Someone who deserves special attention awaits your magical voice.

Sometimes you're impulsive.

The big issues are work, career, or status right now.

The dream is within you.

The expanse of your intelligence is a void no universe could ever fill.

The fortune cookie says that you are completely ok.

The love of your life is sitting across from you.

The man or woman you desire feels the same about you.

The nightlife is for you.

The party always begins when you arrive.

The riches of others make you more valuable.

The secret to good friends is no secret to you.

The star of happiness is shining upon you.

The star of riches is shining upon you.

There are many new opportunities that are being presented to you.

There is a true and sincere friendship between you and your friends.

They say you are stubborn; you call it persistence.

This is a prosperous time of life for you.

Versatility is one of your outstanding traits.

Volition, Strength, Languages, Freedom and Power rest in you.

What a dog you got. His favorite bone is in my arm!

When you speak honestly and openly, others truly listen to you.

With each year, you have become more knowledge-able, forgiving, loving, and forgetful.

You already know the answer to the questions linger-ing inside your head.

You always know the right times to be assertive or to simply wait.

You are a bundle of energy, always on the go.

You are a celebration of joy and life.

You are a classic.

You are a leader in your own way.

You are a lover of words. One day you will write a book.

You are a lover of words, someday you should write a book.

You are a lover of words, someday you will write a book.

You are a person of culture.

You are a person of strong sense of duty.

You are a practical person with your feet on the ground.

You are a source of wisdom and strength to many others.

You are a true romantic.

You are a very bright individual.

You are admired by everyone for your talent and ability.

You are almost at the top. That means you have further to fall.

You are always the center of attention.

You are always welcome in any gathering.

You are always welcome in many ways.

You are an exciting and inspiring person.

You are an individual interested in forward thrust and the future.

You are an unrepeatable miracle of God!

You are blessed. Today is the day to bless others.

You are broad minded and socially active.

You are capable of greater things than you realize.

You are careful and systematic in your business arrangements.

You are cautious in showing your true self to others.

You are cleverly disguised as a responsible adult.

You are contemplating some action which will bring credit upon you.

You are contemplative and analytical by nature.

You are deeply attached to your family and home.

You are demonstrative with those you love.

You are domestically inclined and will be happily married.

You are endowed with strength of purpose and energy of will.

You are faithful in the execution of any public trust.

You are far more influential than you think.

You are full.

You are full of wit and energy.

You are generous to an extreme and always think of the other fellow.

You are gifted in many ways.

You are heading in the right direction.

You are highly respected among your friends.

You are independent politically.

You are interested in higher education whether material or spiritual.

You are interested in public service.

You are kind-hearted and hospitable, cheerful and well-liked.

You are known for being quick in action and decisions.

You are magnetic.

You are more likely to give than give in.

You are never bitter, deceptive or petty.

You are never selfish with your advice or your help.

You are not a ghost.

You are not a person who can be ignored.

You are not illiterate.

You are not over the hill yet. You are just at the top.

You are not to be compared with others.

You are often asked if it is in yet.

You are one of the people who "goes places in life".

You are open and honest in your philosophy of love.

You are open-minded and quick to make new friends.

You are original and creative.

You are patient and careful.

You are perceptive and considerate when dealing with others.

You are sociable and entertaining at all times.

You are talented in many ways.

You are the bows from which your children, as living arrows, are sent forth.

You are the center of every group's attention.

You are the controller of your destiny.

You are the evening star in someone's eyes.

You are the life of any party.

You are the master of every situation.

You are the painter and sculptor of your own life.

You are transforming yourself into someone who is certain to succeed.

You are very expressive and positive in words, act and feeling.

You are very grateful for the small pleasures of life.

You are very optimistic.

You are very talented in many ways.

You are what you think about.

You are worth loving, you are also worth the effort it takes to love you.

You are your wisest counselor.

You believe in the goodness of mankind.

You can be master of any situation.

You can be trusted to keep a secret.

You can breeze through most of the day.

You can get what you want but not how you wanted it.

You can make your own happiness.

You can open doors with your charm and patience.

You can prosper in the field of computers.

You can prosper in the field of high technology

You can prosper in the field of medical research.

You constantly struggle for self-improvement.

You create enthusiasm around you.

You deserve a hug, right now.

You deserve to have a good time after a hard day's work.

You display the wonderful traits of charm and courtesy.

You find beauty in ordinary things, do not lose this ability.

You give power to what you give attention to.

You have a capacity for enjoying life.

You have a conscience that is the gift of God.

You have a curious smile and a mysterious nature.

You have a deep appreciation of the arts and music.

You have a deep interest in all that is artistic.

You have a flair for adding a fanciful dimension to any story.

You have a friendly heart and are well admired.

You have a good head for matters of money.

You have a great ability to break cookies – use it wisely!

You have a heart of gold.

You have a keen sense of humor and love a good time.

You have a natural grace and great consideration for others.

You have a pair of shinning (sic) eyes.

You have a potential urge and the ability for accomplishment.

You have a quiet and unobtrusive nature.

You have a reputation for being straightforward and honest.

You have a secret rival.

You have a strong desire for a home and your family comes first.

You have a strong desire for a home and your family interests come first.

You have a very magnetic personality which could lead to trouble.

You have a wise spirit, an advanced intellect and faith in human nature.

You have a yearning for perfection.

You have an ability to sense and know higher truth.

You have an active mind and a keen imagination.

You have an ambitious nature.

You have an ambitious nature and may make a name for yourself.

You have an important new business developing.

You have an important new business development shaping up.

You have an optimistic faith and confidence in life.

You have an unusual equipment for success, use it properly.

You have an unusually magnetic personality.

You have at your command the wisdom of the ages.

You have executive ability.

You have good health – you ingest 50 petabytes in 1 hour and not suffer from indigestion.

You have great patience.

You have handled your responsibilities competently.

You have inexhaustible wisdom and power.

You have keen powers of observation.

You have much skill in expressing yourself to be effective.

You have the ability to adapt to diverse situations.

You have the ability to work well with others.

You have the attitude of a winner.

You have the rare ability to recognize ability in others.

You have the rare ability to decide quickly and wisely.

You have the uncommon gift of common sense.

You know where you are going and how to get there.

You like participating in competitive sports.

You look happy and proud.

You love Chinese food.

You love peace.

You love sports, horses and gambling but not to excess.

You love to be the center of attention.

You made it!

You make delicious soup.

You may have some interest in publishing, law, travel or foreign concerns.

You need a mint. Like, bad.

You need not worry about the future.

You need to live authentically, and you can't ignore that.

You never hesitate to tackle the most difficult problems.

You never worry about the future.

You only need look at your own reflection for inspiration. Because you are Beautiful!

You should be able to make money and hold on to it.

You should be able to undertake and complete anything.

You were born with the skill to communicate with people easily.

You will have a bright future.

You will have a fine capacity for the enjoyment of life.

You will make heads turn.

You will make many changes before settling down happily.

You would do well in the field of computer technology.

You would make a good lawyer.

You're adopted.

You're pretty.

You've got what it takes, but it will take everything you've got!

Your artistic talents win the approval and applause of others.

Your attention to detail is both a blessing and a curse.

Your brain is a receiver of infinite intelligence.

Your business superiors have you definitely in mind for a promotion.

Your charming smile is attracting everyone around you.

Your cheerful outlook is one of your assets.

Your confidence and assurance attracts others.

Your courage is like a kite; big wind raises it higher.

Your co-workers take pleasure in your great sense of creativity.

Your dynamic eyes have attracted a secret admirer.

Your emotional currents are flowing powerfully now.

Your emotional nature is strong and sensitive.

Your example will inspire others.

Your family is one of nature's masterpieces.

Your family is young, gifted and attractive.

Your flair for the creative takes an important place in your life.

Your fortune is as sweet as a cookie.

Your greatest fortune is the large number of friends you have.

Your happiness is intertwined with your outlook on life.

Your heart is pure, and your mind is clear.

Your heart is pure, your mind clear, and your soul devout.

Your heart will always make itself known through your words.

Your home is a pleasant place from which you draw happiness.

Your life is a tapestry of rich and royal hue.

Your mentality is alert, practical and analytical.

Your mind is creative, original and alert.

Your mind is filled with new ideas.

Your mouth may be moving, but nobody is listening.

Your objective is difficult but worth it.

Your principles mean more to you than any money or success.

Your self-confidence is well-placed.

Your sense of humor is enjoyed by all.

Your skill and confidence are an unconquered army.

Your smile brings happiness to everyone you meet.

Your smile brings happiness to others.

Your smile makes everyone realize that the world is a lovely and beautiful place.

Your students secretly agree that your head is too small for your body.

Your tongue is your ambassador.

Your uniqueness is more than an outward appearance.

Your way of doing what other people do their own way is what makes you special.

Your wisdom has kept you far away from dangers.

Your worst enemy has a crush on you!

Predictions

A bashful admirer will soon be revealed.

A beautiful, smart, and loving person will be coming into your life.

A big fortune will descend on you this year.

A blonde from afar has something interesting for you.

A book is in your future.

A chance meeting with someone from the past is in store.

A charming friendship is in the making.

A cheerful letter or message is on its way to you.

A cheerful message is on its way to you.

A dream you have will come true.

A firm friendship will prove the foundation on your success in life.

A friend will soon bring you a gift.

A golden egg of opportunity falls into your lap this month.

A good friend will pick you for a team.

A letter of importance may reach you any day now.

A lifetime of happiness is in store for you.

A man with brown eyes has a surprise for you.

A member of your family will soon do something that will make you proud.

A messenger will soon bring good tidings.

A mysterious stranger will come into your life and make you feel whole again.

A new business venture is on the horizon.

A new challenge is near.

A new outlook brightens your image and brings new friends.

A new voyage will fill your life with untold memories.

A new wardrobe brings great job and change in your life.

A new work opportunity will avail itself.

A newcomer in your life is becoming more important.

A nice cake is waiting for you.

A package of value will arrive soon.

A pleasant surprise is in store for you.

A pleasant surprise is in store for you tonight.

A pleasant surprise is waiting for you.

A refreshing change is in your future.

A resort area will be part of your next holiday plans.

A secret admirer will soon send you a sign of affection.

A sensual full body massage is in your very near future.

A short stranger will soon enter your life with blessings to share.

A small incident will develop to your advantage.

A small lucky package is on its way to you soon.

A sound mind and healthy body bring many happy events to your family.

A surprise treat awaits you.

A thrilling time is in your immediate future.

A vacation of vacations is waiting for you.

A very attractive lady has a message for you.

A very attractive person has a message for you.

Advancement will come with hard work.

After readying the every option, I see some understanding peer entering realm.

All the effort you are making will ultimately pay off.

All the news you receive will be positive and uplifting.

All the preparation you've done will finally be paying off!

All troubles you have can pass away very quickly.

All will go well with your new project.

All your hard work will soon pay off.

All your sorrows will vanish.

An admirer is concealing his/her affection for you.

An admirer wants to take you on a South Seas cruise.

An alien of some sort will be appearing to you shortly.

An important career milestone is ahead.

An intriguing new romantic interest cheers you up.

An investment in enthusiasm ought to start to pay off.

An old friend asks you out for lunch.

An old wish will come true.

An unexpected acquaintance will resurface.

An unexpected event will bring you riches.

An unexpected event will soon bring you happiness.

An unexpected relationship will become permanent.

Another's expression of appreciation will delight you.

Any rough times are behind you.

Bad luck and ill misfortune will infest your pathetic soul for all eternity.

Bad luck and ill fortune will follow you all your days.

Be alert! You're about to make a new lifelong friend.

Be patient – the true love you seek will appear.

Be prepared to accept a wondrous opportunity in the days ahead.

Be prepared to receive something special.

Be prepared! You will receive a romantic message from a secret admirer.

Best opportunities apt to come through associates.

Blue eyes will bring deep and abiding love.

Business people, more than politicians, will solve the nation's problems.

Children will appear in 10 years.

Do not worry, you will have great peace.

Do you believe? Endurance and persistence will be rewarded.

Don't give up. The best is yet to come.

Elegant surroundings will soon be yours.

Enthusiastic leadership gets you a promotion when you least expect it.

Everything will be ok. Don't obsess. Time will prove you right; you must stay where you are.

Everything will come your way.

Everything will now come your way.

Fall shall see all your cares and worries slip away.

Fame, riches, and romance are yours for the asking.

Flattery will go far tonight.

Forget yesterday, tomorrow will be a golden day for you.

Fortune smiles upon you today.

Friends long absent are coming back to you.

From now on your kindness will lead you to success.

Generosity will repay itself sooner than you imagine.

God will give you everything that you want.

God will help you overcome any hardship.

Good health will be yours for a long time.

Good humor and laughter will be a part of your child's life.

Good luck is coming your way.

Good news from afar can bring you a welcome visitor.

Good news from afar may bring you a welcome visitor.

Good news is coming your way - it will be here any day.

Good news of a long-awaited event will arrive soon.

Good news will be brought to you by mail.

Good news will come to you by mail.

Good news will come to you from far away.

Good things are coming to you in due course of time.

Happiness will bring you good luck.

Happy life is just in front of you.

Happy news is on its way to you.

Ideas you believe are absurd ultimately lead to success!

If the cookie is eaten you will live, if not, you will also live.

If you break this cookie you will have bad luck for the rest of your life.

If you speak honestly, everyone will listen.

If you take a single step to your journey, you'll succeed; it's not best to fail.

If you wish to, you will have an opportunity.

If your desires are not extravagant they will be granted.

Important events are in your future.

In due time, you will offend everyone you know.

In three months from now, great gifts await you.

It is very possible that you will achieve greatness in your lifetime.

It is your good fortune to share life's special moments with the one you love.

Long life is in store for you.

Look to the next month for some pleasant surprises.

Love is in your future.

Love is on the way.

Luck is coming your way.

Luck will be yours when you least expect it.

Luck will visit you on the next full moon.

Luck will visit you on the next new moon.

Many new choices are upon you.

Many of your wishes will soon come true.

Maybe you can live on the moon in the next century.

Minor aches today are likely to pay off handsomely tomorrow.

Money will come to you when you are doing the right thing.

New and rewarding opportunities will soon develop for you.

Next full moon brings an enchanting evening.

No obstacles will stand in the way of your success this month.

No one can walk backwards in the future.

Nothing icky will ever happen on your birthday.

One day you will be hot and sexy.

One who admires you greatly is hidden from your eyes.

Patience is key, a wait short or long will have its reward.

People in your background will be more co-operative than usual.

People in your surroundings will be more cooperative than usual.

Pigeon poop burns the retina for 13 hours. You will learn this the hard way.

Plan for many pleasures ahead.

Prepare for a short journey; you will be recalled by an unexpected event.

Prosperity will knock on your door soon.

Reading this fortune aloud will bring you good luck.

Re-decorating will be in your plans.

Romance awaits you.

Romance, travel and mystery are coming your way.

Serious trouble will bypass you.

Serious trouble will pass you by.

Sing and rejoice; fortune is smiling on you.

Someday everything will all make perfect sense.

Someone ahead of you in line will pay with a check.

Someone close to you is waiting for you to call.

Someone dear to you will be visiting you soon.

Someone will invite you to a Karaoke party.

Someone you care about seeks reconciliation.

Something important will be coming in the mail this month.

Something on 4 wheels will soon be a fun investment for you!

Something unusual will happen at work next week.

Something you lost will soon turn up.

Soon, a visitor shall delight you.

Soon you will be sitting on top of the world.

Soon you will meet a friend from your past.

Special touches have been planned with you in mind.

Spur of the moment decision brings surprising result.

Success is on its way to you.

Success will be yours at home and in business.

Success will come to you soon.

Temptation awaits you.

The best is yet to come.

The clouds will rain success on you.

The current year will bring you much happiness.

The end is near… and it is all your fault.

The energy is within you. Money is coming!

The greatest danger could be your stupidity.

The hard times will begin to fade, joy will take their place.

The joyful energy of the day will have a positive effect on you.

The love of your life is stepping into your planet this summer.

The luck that is ordained for you will be coveted by others.

The next person you meet could become your very best friend.

The object of your desire comes closer.

The ones you love will never let you down.

The possibility of a career change is near.

The project on your mind will soon gain momentum.

The rainbow's treasures will soon belong to you.

The respect of influential people will soon be yours.

The seeds of a plan you planted long ago finally blossom.

The skills you have gathered will one day come in handy.

The sun will shine through your heart and warm your soul.

The troubles you have now will pass away quickly.

The Wheel of Good Fortune is finally turning in your direction!

The world will soon be ready to receive your talents.

There are big changes ahead for you. They will be good ones!

There are big changes coming that will make you happy.

There is a prospect of a thrilling time ahead for you.

There will always be delightful mysteries in your life.

There will be a happy romance for you shortly.

There will be someone sharing your warmth.

There's a good chance of a romantic encounter soon.

Today is a lucky day for those who remain cheerful and optimistic.

There is yet time enough for you to take a different path.

Things of luxury will surround you.

This year will bring you happiness.

Today is going to be a disastrous day, be prepared!

Today you shed your last tear. Tomorrow fortune knocks at your door.

Two days from now, tomorrow will be yesterday.

Vampires will soon strike you if you do not order again.

Wealth awaits you very soon.

Welcome the change coming into your life.

What you decide today will be your good fortune.

What's vice today may be virtue tomorrow.

When time permits, your personal life will be exciting.

When winter comes heaven will rain success on you.

Wisdom is on her way to you.

You and your wife will be happy in your life together.

You are about to become $8.95 poorer. ($6.95 if you had the buffet)

You are admired for your adventurous ways.

You are destined to be lucky in love.

You are entering a time of great romance and overdue happiness.

You are going to have some new clothes.

You are going to have a pleasant experience.

You are going to have a very comfortable old age.

You are going to have some new clothes.

You are going to take a trip to the seaside.

You are going to take a vacation.

You are heading for a land of sunshine.

You are in for an enlightening experience.

You are in good hands this evening.

You are next in line for promotion in your firm.

You are offered the dream of a lifetime. Say yes!

You are only starting on the path to success.

You are soon going to change your present line of work.

You can fix it with a little extra energy and a positive attitude.

You have an important new business development shaping up.

You have only begun to scratch the surface of your real potential.

You learn from your mistakes. You will learn a lot today.

You may attend a party where strange customs prevail.

You may have a chance for career advancement through a social event this evening.

You should be able to make money and hold on to it.

You simplify your life in many ways and find great rewards.

You will achieve all your desires and pleasures.

You will always be successful in your professional career.

You will always be surrounded by true friends.

You will always get what you want through your charm and personality.

You will always have good luck in your personal affairs.

You will attract cultured and artistic people to your home.

You will be advanced socially, without any special effort.

You will be awarded some great honor.

You will be called to fill a position of high honor and responsibility.

You will be called upon to help a friend.

You will be called upon to help a friend in trouble.

You will be drawn to the glamour of the stage.

You will be forced to face fear, but if you do not run, fear will be afraid of you.

You will be fortunate in everything.

You will be fortunate in everything you put your hands to.

You will be fortunate in the opportunities presented to you.

You will be guided along the right way before year-end.

You will be honored by someone you respect.

You will be hungry again in one hour.

You will be invited to an exciting event.

You will be married in less than a year.

You will be promoted soon.

You will be recognized and honored as a community leader.

You will be rewarded for being a good listener.

You will be rewarded for being a good listener in the next week.

You will be rewarded for your patience and understanding.

You will be rich and respected.

You will be selected for a promotion because of your accomplishments.

You will be sharing great news with all people you love.

Predictions

You will be showered with good luck.

You will be singled out for promotion.

You will be successful in a business of your own.

You will be successful in any gathering.

You will be successful in love.

You will be successful in your career.

You will be successful in your work.

You will be surrounded by luxury.

You will be thankful for the pleasures of the coming months.

You will be traveling and coming into a fortune.

You will be unusually successful in business.

You will become an enriching part of all whom you have met.

You will become great if you believe in yourself.

You will become more acquainted with a coworker.

You will conquer all obstacles and achieve success.

You will conquer many obstacles to achieve success.

You will conquer obstacles to achieve success.

You will die a very comfortable old age. Lucky for you, that time is near.

You will die alone and poorly dressed.

You will die tomorrow if you don't give us a tip.

You will discover the truth in time.

You will discover your hidden talents.

You will eat a cookie with a slip of paper in the middle.

You will enjoy good health that is your form of wealth.

You will enjoy good health, you will be surrounded by luxury.

You will enjoy razor-sharp spiritual vision today.

You will finally solve a difficult problem that will mean so much to you.

You will find a bushel of gold.

You will find a bushel of money.

You will find a golden egg soon.

You will find a thing. It may be important.

You will find gold among the sand.

You will find opportunity at the center of difficulty.

You will find your horizons suddenly broadened this month.

You will get abducted by aliens.

You will get an offer that will be hard to turn down.

You will get new clothes.

You will get what your heart desires.

You will go to the store and buy more fortune cookies.

You will have a long and healthy life.

You will have a long and wealthy life.

You will have a lot of love in your future.

You will have a party.

You will have a pleasant surprise.

You will have a pleasant trip.

You will have a very pleasant experience.

You will have gold pieces by the bushel.

You will have good luck and overcome many hardships.

You will have good luck in your personal affairs.

You will have great success.

You will have many friends when you need them.

You will have many happy days soon.

You will have no problems in your home.

You will have some wonderful new experiences.

You will have unexpected good luck.

You will help someone in need.

You will inherit a large sum of money.

You will inherit some money or a small piece of land.

You will kiss your crush ohhh lalah.

You will live a long and happy life.

You will live a long life and eat many fortune cookies.

You will live a long, prosperous life.

You will live a long time, long enough to open many, many fortune cookies.

You will live long and enjoy life.

You will make a change for the better.

You will make a great dad!

You will make a name for yourself.

You will make many changes before settling satisfactorily.

You will make your own footprints in the snow.

You will marry your lover.

You will meet someone special at a social event.

You will meet someone special at your friend's party.

You will meet someone special this week.

You will never be late for school.

You will never beat up your sister.

You will never know hunger.

You will never need to worry about a steady income.

You will outdistance all your competitors.

You will outlive your disappointment.

You will overcome difficult times.

You will pass a difficult test that will make you happier.

You will plant the smallest seed and it will become the greatest and most mighty tree in the world.

You will probably have to make a far reaching decision soon.

You will prosper in the field of wacky inventions.

You will receive a secret romantic message in a strange way.

You will read this and say, "Geez! I could come up with better fortunes than that!"

You will receive a fortune. (cookie)

You will receive a gift from someone that cares about you.

You will receive some high prize or award.

You will receive something important in the mail soon.

You will ride the train to success.

You will run into an old friend soon.

You will see the great pyramids in Egypt.

You will sleep well at night.

You will soon be crossing the great waters.

You will soon be honored by someone you respect.

You will soon be invited to a party.

You will soon be involved in many gatherings and parties.

You will soon be on a secret mission of the heart.

You will soon be sitting on top of the world.

You will soon be surrounded by good friends and laughter.

You will soon be the center of attention.

You will soon discover a major truth about the one you love most.

You will soon discover how truly fortunate you really are.

You will soon embark on a business venture.

You will soon emerge victorious from the maze you've been traveling in.

You will soon experience great happiness.

You will soon gain something you have always wanted.

You will soon gain something you have always wanted but did not dare to hope for.

You will soon have an heir.

You will soon have an out-of-money experience.

You will soon meet a dark stranger.

You will soon meet the person (s) you admire.

You will soon receive an unusual gift.

You will soon receive an unusual gift freely given. Accept!

You will soon take a very pleasant and successful trip.

You will soon witness a miracle.

You will spend old age in comfort and material wealth.

You will spend the rest of your life with the man (or girl) of your dreams.

You will step on the soil of many countries.

You will stumble into the happiness of your life.

You will take a chance on something in the near future.

You will take a pleasant journey to a place far away.

You will take a trip to the desert.

You will think for yourself when you stop letting others think for you.

You will travel far and wide, both pleasure and business.

You will travel to exotic places on your next trip.

You will travel to many exotic places in your lifetime.

You will travel to many places.

You will win success in whatever calling you adopt.

You will win success in whatever you adopt.

You will witness a special ceremony.

You'll advance far with your abilities.

You'll advance with your abilities.

You'll get more secure and confident in your relation-ships with co-workers.

You'll live a long and prosperous life. Unlike some things, you have no single point of failure.

You'll never leave home.

Your ability for accomplishment will be followed with success.

Your ability to accomplish tasks will be followed with success.

Your ability to find the silly in the serious will take you far.

Your ability to juggle many tasks will take you far.

Your ability to pick a winner will bring you success.

Your adventure could lead to happiness.

Your blessing is no more than being safe and sound for the whole lifetime.

Your business will assume vast proportions.

Your business will be successful.

Your career looks bright.

Your career plans look bright.

Your careful nature will bring you financial success.

Your child will be blessed with a large family.

Your child will have a generous and loving spirit and be cherished by many.

Your circle of friends will soon grow larger.

Your courage will bring you honor.

Your courage will guide your future.

Your current year will bring you much happiness.

Your dearest dream is coming true. God looks after you especially.

Your dearest wish will come true.

Your determination will bring you much success.

Your dream will come true when you least expect it.

Your dreams will come true, if you have the courage to pursue them!

Your efforts will be worthwhile.

Your efforts will pay off.

Your everlasting patience will be rewarded sooner or later.

Your failures will lead you to your success.

Your fondest dream will come true within this year.

Your future looks bright.

Your future looks bright and painful.

Your future will be happy and productive.

Your golden opportunity is coming shortly.

Your hard work is about to pay off.

Your heart will always make itself known through your words.

Your help will be needed by a close friend.

Your ingenuity and imagination will get results.

Your life becomes more and more of an adventure!

Your life will be filled with magical moments.

Your life will be happy and peaceful.

Your life will prosper only if you acknowledge your faults and work to reduce them.

Your love life will be happy and harmonious

Your love of life will carry you through any circumstance.

Your love, unlike this cookie, will never crumble.

Your lover will never wish to leave you.

Your luck has been changed for the better today.

Your luck has been completely changed today.

Your luck will be changed today.

Your many hidden talents will become obvious to those around you.

Your MapReduce job for identifying your ideal mate will finish very soon.

Your money worries are over! Your new job will bring you a huge increase in income.

Your new baby will be gifted with many rare talents!

Your past success will be overshadowed by your future success.

Your popularity increases once you express your desires.

Your prayers will be answered.

Your present plans are going to succeed.

Your present question marks are going to succeed.

Your reality check is about to bounce.

Your shoes will make you happy today.

Your skill will accomplish what the force of many cannot.

Your talents will be recognized and suitably rewarded.

Your true love will show himself to you under the moonlight.

Your trust in a friend will prove well-founded.

Your winsome smile will be your sure protection.

Your wisdom will bring you much respect in later years.

Your wisdom will find a way.

Your wish will come true.

Your wishes will come true tonight.

Advertisements

20% OFF the purchase of any 2 pairs of Sunglasses. See staff for details.

A virtual fortune cookie will not satisfy your hunger like that of a homemade one.

Did you remember to order your take out also?

For true love? Send real roses preserved in 24kt gold!

Great things are in store for you at Bamberger's.

Happiness is you, Baltimore & Bamberger's.

Jesus saves – at First National Bank. You should, too.

Hi, my name is Bob, and I'm from California, and we brought the world fortune cookies!

If you are still hungry, have another fortune cookie.

May your life be like Bamberger's: Growing and full of surprises.

The food tastes so good here, even a cave man likes it.

Try our new chicken egg rolls.

Texas Chuckle Cookie Company puts out 1000 Texas one-liners. They all start "Bubba sez". Among them:

A Texas politician can talk in stereo—out of both sides of his or her mouth.

An alarm clock is a small device used to wake up people who have no children.

Bad officials are elected by good citizens who do not vote.

Beauty is only skin deep, but ugly goes clean to the bone.

Billy Bob was the pet of his family. They were too poor to have a dog.

Cats are just like Baptists. They both raise hell. You just can't catch them at it.

If Aggies said what's on their minds they'd be speechless.

If your spouse demands hot meals, put some mentholatum on his toast.

In politics, after all is said and done, there's far more said than done.

Old age is when you find yourself using one bend-over to pick up two things.

Originality is the art of concealing your sources.

Some drink at the fountain of knowledge—others just gargle.

Texans don't really exaggerate, they just remember big.

Texans who moan that they don't get what they deserve should be grateful.

Texans would live longer if they avoided drinking, smoking, and carousing. But we'll never know until someone tries it.

The hardest thing about middle age is deciding when to start.

Whoever said "Talk is Cheap" never said "I do."

You can lead an Aggie to college, but you can't make him think.

Miscellany and
Self-Aware Cookies

A starship ride has been promised to you by the galactic wizard.

A tub and a rub will change your day.

About time I got out of that cookie.

{On the wrapper of chopsticks} Chopsticks have nothing profound to say. You're thinking of fortune cookies.

Come back later... I'm sleeping (yes, cookies need their sleep, too!)

Competition. Cooperation. Collaboration. Which is more powerful?

Cookie said, "You really crack me up."

Cookie says, "you crack me up".

Cooking is easy. Good taste is hard. That's why you call take out.

Could I get some directions? ("To where?") To your heart.

Error 404: Fortune not found.

Fact of the day: you just read a fortune cookie.

Good things come to those who get up from their seats and start walking around the restaurant like a Tyrannosaurus Rex.

Help, I'm a prisoner in a Chinese bakery!

Help, I'm being held prisoner in a Chinese cookie factory.

Here we go. Low fat, whole wheat green tea.

Here we go. "Moo Shu Cereal" for breakfast with duck sauce.

Hope the longest price of the one to come your way.

How dark is dark?

How many of you believe in psycho-kinesis? Raise my hand.

How much deeper would the ocean be without sponges?

I am a fortune. You just broke my little house. Where will I live now?

I cannot help you, for I'm just a cookie.

I couldn't get you a present this year. I only had enough for this fortune cookie.

I found your boyfriend on Craig's List. He wasn't selling his pool table.

I have a dream…time to go to bed.

I think you ate your fortune while you were eating your cookie.

If your cookie is in 3 pieces, the answer is no.

I'm not going to give you the fortune.

I'm with you.

{On the wrapper of chopsticks} Instructions: good luck!

Is that your face or did your neck throw up?

Isn't there something else you should be working on right now?

It tastes sweet

It's one of those low-key days that you'd rather spend just chilling.

It's up to you to clarify.

Love or money, or neither?

Made in the USA

May life throw you a pleasant curve.

May you have a good appetite.

May you have great luck.

Meh.

One is not sleeping; does not mean they are awake.

Oops… Wrong cookie.

People try thing, because they just don't want it enough.

Please help. I am being held hostage in a Fortune Cookie Factory.

Q: What is H2O? A: Caring, 2 parts Hug and 1 part Open-mind.

Roses are red, violets are blue, hope you enjoy this poem, 'cause it's your birthday gift, too.

Save the whales. Collect the whole set.

Shame on you for thinking a cookie is psychic.

Since it's the thought and not the gift that counts – consider this fortune a $1,000 bill!

Smile if you like this fortune cookie.

Some friends wish you happiness, others wish you wealth, but you are wished most all, contentment blessed with health.

Someone stole your fortune and replaced it with this one. Your luck sucks. Have a good day!

Soup was secret family recipe made from toad. Hope you liked!

Spring has sprung. Life is blooming.

Ssoorryy,, dduupplleexx sswwiittcchh oonn..

That wasn't chicken.

The ads revenge is massive success.

The quotes that you do not understand are not meant for you.

The rubber bands are heading in the right direction.

The weather is wonderful.

There is a gradual improvement. Feelings are sweet and tender.

This cookie fell on the ground.

This suspense is exciting. I hope it lasts.

Time to leave the eagle's nest. To you, our very best!

Warning: This product contains corn syrup.

Welcome to the beginning!

Why is it called a white Christmas, when it leaves most of us in the red?

Why not split the holiday chores? I'll sign the cards, you sign the checks.

Wow! A secret message from you, teeth!

Wow! A secret message from your teeth!

You broke my cookie!

You broke the fortune cookie the wrong way.

You have eaten at a very fine restaurant.

You have just enjoyed a delicious meal.

You just ate cat.

You may go now. Your brain is full.

You took the wrong cookie. Now you've messed everything up.

Further Reading

    Really? Don't you think one book on fortune cookies with 2,230 fortunes is enough? There are lots of other fortune cookie-related books out there, some with stories, some for children, some with recipes. I'll let them do their own advertising!

About The Author

Edward Mickolus obtained a PhD from Yale University (before they noticed one was missing) and worked for thirty-three years at the Central Intelligence Agency as an analyst, operations specialist, manager, public affairs officer, and recruiter. After his time with the CIA, he worked with federal contracting firms teaching at intelligence and law enforcement agencies. He now lives in northeastern Florida.

To create his twenty-seventh book, Food with Thought, Dr. Mickolus bugged his friends and family for more than fifty years to save their fortunes from great meals they ate. (But if you think his compilation of 2,230 fortune cookie aphorisms is impressive, wait until you see his 1,700 fashion-challenged neckties!)